THE OFFICIAL
LIVERPOOL F

ANNUAL 2005

YOU'LL NEVER WALK ALONE

LIVERPOOL
FOOTBALL CLUB

EST·1892

CONTENTS

THE OFFICIAL
LIVERPOOL FC
ANNUAL 2005

ALL STATISTICS CORRECT AS OF 1ST JUNE 2004

BRIAL...

LFC'S PUBLIC RELATIONS MANAGER BRIAN HALL PLAYED 224 GAMES IN EIGHT SEASONS FOR THE REDS

You'll never walk alone

+ + + 70S STARS BRIAN HALL AND STEVE HEIGHWAY WERE BOTH AMATEURS WHEN INVITED TO THE CLUB FOR TRIALS + + +

WHICH MAKES HIM A GOOD JUDGE OF WHY THE CLUB IS SO SPECIAL

Brian Hall next to Ray Clemence after the 1974 Cup Final

This season is vital for the club if we want to take our place among the top clubs in the English game once more.

The challenge is on to re-establish ourselves as genuine contenders for the Premiership title, as well as to progress in the Champions League.

We should always remember that, within the context of Liverpool Football Club, the league championship is and always has been the prime target. The campaign in Europe is brilliant, but the main thing we are going for is the title. Traditionally that has always been our bread and butter.

When you think about it, these really are exciting times: we have a new manager, some terrific players and there are new strategies in place to bring us success. In other words, we have a great opportunity to move the club forward.

When I was a player, there was nothing like running out on to the pitch at Anfield, even when you were playing for the reserves.

Pack the place with 45,000 people and the noise which hit you when you ran out of the players' tunnel was unbelievable. The buzz was incredible. There's no place quite like Anfield and nobody quite like Liverpool fans. They have their own songs, their own sense of humour and their own way of doing things. The club owes them everything. That's why we always try to give something back to the people of Merseyside.

Everyone at the club is very aware of the fact that the club isn't just famous on Merseyside but all over the world – it is an enormous source of pride.

One of the things about LFC that hasn't changed in all the years that I have been fortunate enough to be associated with it, going back to 1965, is the togetherness, the sense of family and the feeling of belonging that everyone who works for the football club shares with the supporters.

We all feel this togetherness – we are in this for one reason and one reason alone and that is to win football matches. That's why whenever I hear 'You'll Never Walk Alone', the hair still stands up on the back of my neck.

England's finest

STEVEN GERRARD HAS GOT THE LOT: TACTICAL AWARENESS, ENDLESS ENERGY, SKILL TO BURN AND THE PRICELESS ABILITY TO SCORE MATCH-WINNING GOALS

Steven Gerrard has admitted he wants to spend the rest of his career as Liverpool captain.

Gerrard was handed the armband during the early stages of last season and went on to enjoy his best campaign so far, as he drove the Reds towards a top-four finish during a turbulent year.

Already rated as one of the best midfielders in the game, the locally-born star has admitted he would love nothing better than to see out his playing days representing the team he supported avidly as a youngster.

"I love Liverpool and I always have done," he says. "For me this is the best club in the world and to be the captain really is a dream come true.

"I always wanted to be Liverpool captain but I really didn't think it would happen so quickly for me. When Gerard Houllier told me he wanted me to be his new skipper I couldn't believe it. I was very happy.

"To be honest I think I have developed as a player in the time I have been the captain. The extra responsibility has done me the world of good. I knew there were areas of my game that I had to improve on and I feel as though I am doing okay. It's good when people say

nice things about me and say I am doing well, but really it's all about looking forward and setting new standards for the future.

"People have spoken about me in the same breath as Roy Keane and Patrick Vieira but, to be honest, I don't think I'm at their level yet. It's nice to hear those sort of compliments but I think I have a way to go to get to their standard. Whenever they are playing I always follow their performances closely because they are both top class. They set the standards I want to reach."

One man who isn't slow to praise Gerrard is former manager Gerard Houllier.

The Reds' ex-boss says Steven has all the attributes to become one of the biggest stars in the game – but he insists there is no room for complacency.

Houllier says, "Steven is a big player, a top player. But he can become even better. I like the way he reacted to becoming captain.

STEVIE'S STATS FOR CLUB AND COUNTRY UP TO MAY 2004

1ST TEAM GAMES	**240**
1ST TEAM GOALS	**27**
ENGLAND CAPS	**20**
ENGLAND GOALS	**3**

This year, Gerrard also wore the captain's armband for England v Sweden

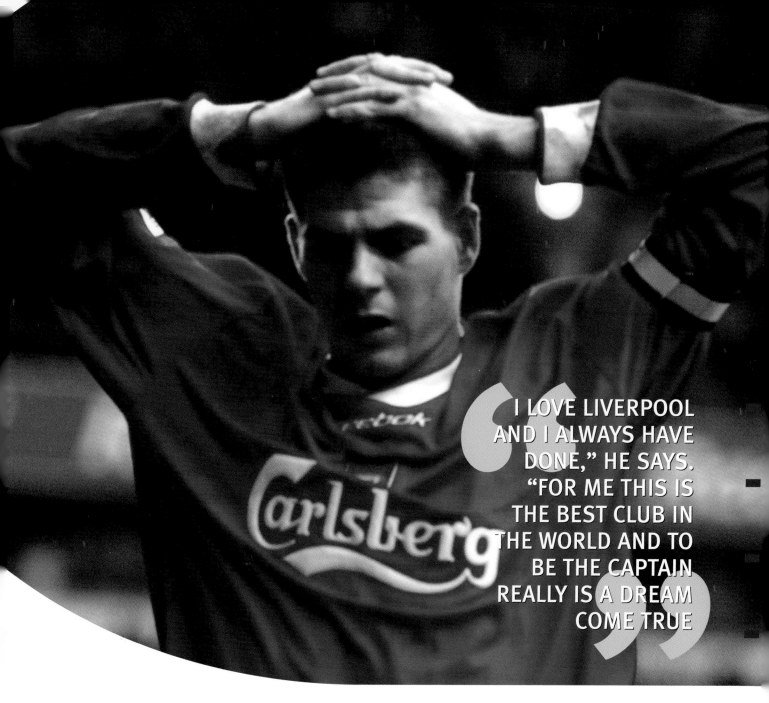

"I LOVE LIVERPOOL AND I ALWAYS HAVE DONE," HE SAYS. "FOR ME THIS IS THE BEST CLUB IN THE WORLD AND TO BE THE CAPTAIN REALLY IS A DREAM COME TRUE"

"His game has taken on an extra edge and he is a shining example to the rest of the players.

"Look at his record for the international team to see how important he is. When he plays for England they very rarely lose.

"He is a top-class player now but the target for him is to become a world-class player. He's not at that level yet, but he can get there. Remember he is still young and still learning the game. The future is very bright for him."

Gerrard wants a future rewarded with silverware and winner's medals – and he hopes he can fulfil his ambitions at Liverpool.

He says, "I signed a new contract last year because I am confident this club is going in the right direction. There's no doubt about that in my mind.

"We have a good group of players and a lot of quality within the squad. There's no reason at all why we can't be challenging with the top teams in the country.

"It's important for me on a personal level to be playing at the top and I see no reason why that can't be the case at Liverpool. I want to be challenging for the title every year and playing in the Champions League every year. They are realistic goals at this club.

"As captain I feel the responsibility

to make sure the club is doing well. If I think players need a rollicking during a match then I'm not afraid to do it. I like to think the lads respect me as a captain.

"There's no doubt that last season was a disappointing one. We didn't win any trophies and the best league position we could aim for was fourth. That really isn't good enough for this club and I know we're all determined this year to make a big improvement."

Gerrard is a player on an upward curve: he can look back with satisfaction and see how his game has progressed, but he knows there is more to come. He wants to win the Premiership title, and he wants to do it with Liverpool. ✦

"IT'S NO SECRET THAT MANCHESTER UNITED WERE KEEN ON SIGNING ME AS WELL BUT I FELT I WANTED TO MOVE TO A CLUB ON THE UP RATHER THAN TO ONE WHICH HAD BEEN AT THE TOP RECENTLY AND COULD BE GOING INTO A DECLINE"

HARRY'S STATS FOR CLUB AND COUNTRY UP TO MAY 2004

1ST TEAM GAMES	49
1ST TEAM GOALS	11
AUSTRALIA CAPS	15
AUSTRALIA GOALS	7

aussie rules ok

HARRY KEWELL HAD HIS PICK OF THE WORLD'S LEADING CLUBS WHEN HE DECIDED TO LEAVE LEEDS UNITED BUT THERE WAS ONLY ONE DESTINATION FOR THE MAN FROM DOWN UNDER

Harry Kewell had the choice of many of Europe's top clubs when he decided to leave Leeds United – but what swung the decision in Liverpool's favour?

"They were the club which impressed me most and Gerard Houllier was the manager who told me what I wanted to hear," says the Aussie star.

Exactly what Houllier said to entice Kewell to Anfield will remain a mystery, but Liverpool's number seven has no doubts he made the right decision.

"Everything about this club is just perfect," he says. "The attention to detail, the preparation for matches, the coaching, the players, the training, everything is first-class.

"As soon as I spoke to Gerard Houllier I knew Liverpool was the right club for me. Of course it was a wrench to leave Leeds because I had lots of good times there, but at that stage of my career I felt it was right to move on.

"Gerard excited me. He said he had a plan for where he wanted to use me and that did excite me a great deal. I wasn't going to be a player stuck in one position. I don't like to play just one role. I feel I can operate in a number of areas, whether it be across midfield, behind the strikers or up front. I can contribute to a team in many ways.

"It's no secret that Manchester United were keen on signing me as well but I felt I wanted to move to a club on the up rather than to one which had been at the top recently and could be going into a decline. The challenge at Liverpool excited me and nothing that has happened since I came here has made me doubt I made the right decision."

If Liverpool excited Kewell, then Kewell certainly excited Liverpool fans. Voted the Most Exciting Signing since John Barnes on the club's official website, the Aussie star's arrival certainly gave Reds fans a timely boost just a few weeks after they suffered the agony of failing to qualify for the Champions League at Chelsea.

"It's nice to know the fans were pleased to see me at Liverpool," says Kewell. "I have always enjoyed playing at Anfield and, of course, Liverpool supporters are well-known all over the world. They make you feel special as a player and that's certainly the reception I got when I made my debut.

"The most exciting signing for years? That's quite a compliment. I hope I can live up to that billing and consistently produce the goods over time.

"There was a bit of a cloud on the day the signing was announced because of the fee Leeds got for me and that disappointed me. Signing for the club you have always supported should be a special day, a perfect day, but it didn't

happen like that for me. There was a bit of a bad taste in the mouth because of some of the things Leeds were saying, but that was their problem and not mine.

"As far as I was concerned I gave them many years of good service. I showed loyalty to them over a long period of time, but I just felt the opportunity to move to a bigger club was one that I couldn't refuse."

Kewell made an instant impact at Anfield, reaching double figures in goals scored during his debut season.

"Scoring goals is a big part of my game," he says. "I'm always a bit disappointed if I don't contribute a decent share over the course of a season.

"I'll never forget my first derby goal when we won 3–0 at Goodison. That was special because of what it meant to the fans. I'll never forget that moment when the ball hit the back of the net.

"I wouldn't say I was consistently on top of my game last season. I had one or two injury problems which held me back a bit, but I feel as though I did pretty well for a first season.

"I'm excited by the future at Liverpool. We have a great squad with great players and we can only get better.

"People may have wondered why I chose Liverpool ahead of other clubs but I know in my mind that I made the right decision. I know I'll win trophies here in time."

H A R R Y   K E W E L L

THE RED BADGE OF COURAGE

Think of Liverpool Football Club and your first thoughts might be of the greatest players or the greatest managers we have been proud to be associated with over the years.

On the other hand you might think of the world-famous Kop, the anthem 'You'll Never Walk Alone' or the well-known wit and humour of Liverpool fans – the greatest in the world.

You'll probably also think of the Liver Bird – the symbol of the club which is featured on the crest. The

'Liver Bird' is an imaginary cross between an eagle and a cormorant. When Liverpool was granted city status by King John, an impression of the Liver Bird was incorporated into the wax which sealed the charter. Ever since, the Liver Bird has become a traditional symbol of the City of Liverpool and is therefore an integral part of the badge of Liverpool FC.

Liverpool has three Liver Birds, two at the Pier Head standing proud on top of the Royal Liver Buildings. Legend has it that they protect the city by keeping watch

at night. They are 18 feet tall, and have a 24-ft wing span. They are made from heavily-gilded, hammered copper. The third is on Mersey Chambers by St Nicholas' Parish Church, and is half the size.

In addition, 'You'll Never Walk Alone' is the famous anthem of the Club. The current logo incorporates this motto along with a representation of the iron curlicues of the 'Shankly Gates'. The flame on the badge honours the memory of the 96 Liverpool supporters who died in the Hillsborough tragedy of 1989.

The iron curlicues of the 'Shankly Gates' are recreated at the top of the Liverpool FC badge

YOU'LL NEVER WALK ALONE

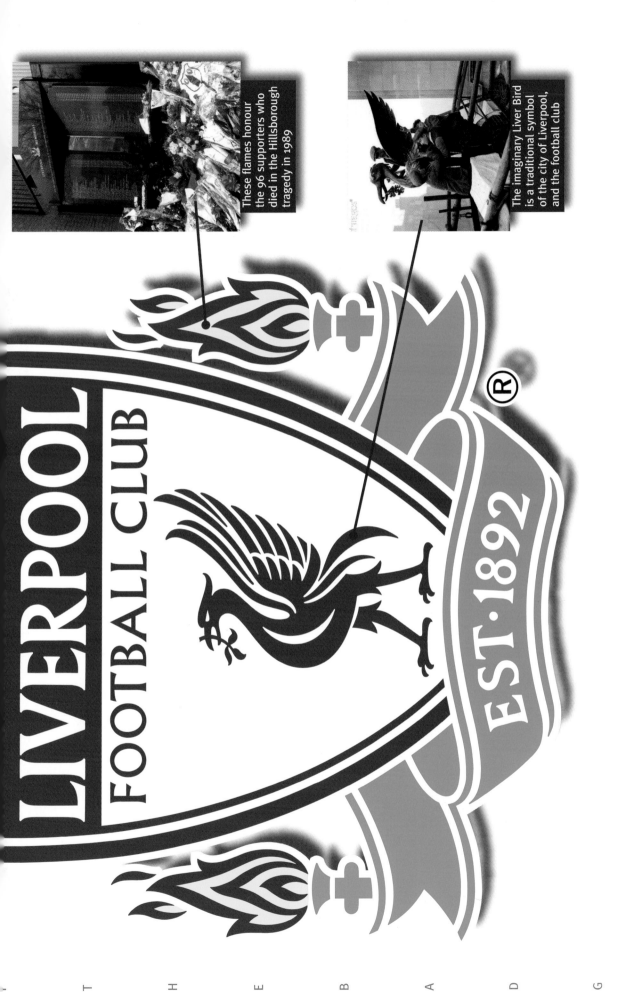

These flames honour the 96 supporters who died in the Hillsborough tragedy in 1989

The imaginary Liver Bird is a traditional symbol of the city of Liverpool, and the football club

LIVERPOOL FOOTBALL CLUB

EST·1892

®

T H E B A D G E

MICHAEL'S TOP TEN

FA CUP WINNER V ARSENAL

It was the goal which won Liverpool their second trophy on the way to an unprecedented Treble in 2001. After Owen had cancelled out Freddie Ljungberg's opener for Arsenal in Cardiff's Millennium Stadium, it appeared as if the Cup Final was heading for 30 minutes of extra-time.

But Liverpool had other ideas and sealed a famous victory with just minutes to go, thanks to the goalscoring instincts of their star striker. When Patrik Berger sent a looping ball over the Arsenal defence, it was Owen who reacted quickest to control possession on the left side of the area. After beating Martin Keown, he aimed low for the far corner of David Seaman's goal and sent 30,000 Liverpool fans at that same end of the ground into ecstasy as the ball nestled neatly inside the post. Whoever said Michael couldn't use his left foot?

ROMAN EMPEROR

February 15 2001 will go down as one of Liverpool's finest-ever away performances in Europe. Having travelled to the Olympic Stadium in Rome for the first leg, the ground that staged two of their four European Cup triumphs, Liverpool put on a wonderfully disciplined display as they achieved one of the best results by an English club against top-class opposition away from home. And they had Michael Owen to thank for their victory with two world-class goals.

The first arrived after 46 minutes following a mistake in the Roma defence. Rinaldi tried to play a cross-field pass over Owen, only for the England striker to bring the ball down and hit a sweet right-foot shot into the corner to the delight of the 4,000 travelling Liverpool fans. And the second arrived following more indecision in the Roma defence which allowed Christian Ziege time to drive down the right, and from his skilful centre Owen beat his marker at the near post to head home.

A great result for Liverpool thanks to a world-class performance from their number one striker, and the team later marched on to lift the UEFA Cup.

MICHAEL OWEN

■ GEORDIES PUT TO THE SWORD

Who will ever forget Owen's cheeky 'rubbing hands' celebration as he wheeled away in delight after completing a brilliant hat-trick against Newcastle at St James Park in 1998–99? England's boy wonder had just grabbed yet another match ball with a quite simply brilliant display of goalscoring in the North-East. If his first two goals were good, then his third was breathtaking. Showing a maturity beyond his tender years, Owen picked the ball up just inside the Newcastle half before charging forward on a run the great Maradona would have been proud of. Once he had got beyond the last man and had just the keeper to beat, he clipped a shot with the outside of his right foot which drifted inside the far post. A brilliant goal!

CARDIFF GLORY

It was a goal no Liverpool fan will ever forget as Michael Owen secured a famous victory over Manchester United in March 2003 to land the Worthington Cup in Cardiff. Steven Gerrard had given Liverpool a first-half lead with a deflected shot, but the Reds were hanging on in the closing minutes as United pressed for the equaliser. Their hopes were dashed when Liverpool hit them on the break late in the game to win the Cup. Didi Hamann slid Owen in behind the United defence, giving him all the time in the world to choose his spot. With only Barthez to beat, Owen drilled the ball hard and low into the far corner to give Kopites another famous day to enjoy in the Welsh capital.

DEBUT DELIGHT

He was a fresh-faced 17–year-old when he made his first-team debut for Roy Evans' Liverpool at a cold Selhurst Park back in 1997. Much had been written about Owen's scoring displays for the reserves and youth teams before Evans decided the time was right to give him a chance on the big stage. He took it in magical fashion, netting his first goal for Liverpool shortly after coming off the subs' bench with a neat finish into the corner of the goal after the Reds had created space for him inside the penalty area. He was clearly about to live up to his pre-debut billing as the brightest young talent in English football.

EURO RECORD-BREAKER

Michael Owen's header in the European outpost of Ljubljana in Slovenia last season may not be one of the greatest goals in Liverpool's illustrious history in continental football – but it was a personal landmark for the striking ace. When the ball flew into the Olimpija Ljubljana net in the second half of the 1–1 draw, it was his 21st goal in Europe for Liverpool and made him the club's top goalscorer in European competition. Not bad going for a 23-year-old. And, for the record, the historic strike came in his 45th European game for Liverpool.

HAT-TRICK HERO

One of the greatest days in the history of English football got off to a bad start when Carsten Jancker put Germany 1–0 up against England in a World Cup qualifier in Munich in September 2001. Then the Liverpool contingent got busy. Owen scored, then Gerrard, then Owen again and, in the 66th minute, Owen got his hat-trick with a fine finish after being put through by Steven Gerrard. That left Emile Heskey to round things off with a goal that left the ex-World Champions on their knees. Germany 1, Liverpool 5.

FA CUP EQUALISER V ARSENAL

Liverpool had quite simply been torn apart by Arsenal in the 2001 Cup final before Michael Owen decided to take matters into his own hands. Seven minutes from time, the Gunners seemed set for a deserved 1–0 victory before Owen levelled the game with a well-executed volley to give Gerard Houllier's men renewed hope in their Treble push. When Arsenal failed to clear the danger inside their area, the ball broke for Owen who connected sweetly on the half-volley to fire into the corner of the net.

TON-UP OWEN

It was in December 2001 when Owen reached a century of goals for Liverpool. Four years after breaking onto the scene, Owen joined an elite group of players to have notched a ton of goals for the Reds. The Reds were a goal down with just two minutes left to play at West Ham, when Emile Heskey diverted the ball into Owen's path and the young striker made no mistake with a rasping volley into the roof of the net.

THAT GOAL FOR ENGLAND

No Michael Owen goals tribute would be complete without mention of the strike which made him a household name throughout world football.

It came in the white of England, on a mild afternoon in St Etienne as Glenn Hoddle's men took on Argentina in a 1998 World Cup clash. Owen terrorised the Argentine defence and scored the goal of the tournament when he left defenders trailing in his wake before blasting the ball into the the goal. In that one moment, Michael Owen ensured his life would never be the same again.

MICHAEL OWEN

+ + + MICHAEL OWEN WAS NOT GIVEN A RED OR EVEN A YELLOW CARD IN ANY COMPETITION DURING THE LAST THREE SEASONS + + +

O W E N

2003

↘ NEW SIGNINGS HARRY KEWELL, STEVE FINNAN, ANTHONY LE TALLEC AND FLORENT SINAMA PONGOLLE WERE UNVEILED AT ANFIELD AS GERARD HOULLIER'S FOUR SUMMER SIGNINGS FOR THE NEW SEASON. KEWELL, AT £5 MILLION, WAS THE TRANSFER COUP LIVERPOOL FANS HAD BEEN HOPING FOR SINCE SPECULATION ABOUT HIS ARRIVAL FIRST BEGAN TO SURFACE DURING THE SUMMER

2004

→

AUGUST 17 2003

Liverpool kick off the season with a disappointing 2–1 home defeat to Roman Abramovich's Chelsea. Juan Sebastian Veron and Jimmy Floyd Hasselbaink are on target for the newly-wealthy Londoners as Michael Owen nets a consolation for the Reds with a re-taken penalty. It is the first time Liverpool have lost their opening game at home since 1962.

AUGUST 24 + 30 2003

Liverpool pick up their first point of the season with a goalless draw at Villa Park. John Arne Riise goes close to winning it for the Reds in the final minute with a flying header. The first victory arrives on August 30, as the Reds trounce Everton 3–0 at Goodison Park to get the season up and running. Harry Kewell is among the scorers as he celebrates his first goal for his new club. Gerard Houllier is left celebrating the fact he's the first manager in Liverpool history to win four games in a row at Everton.

SEPTEMBER 13 2003

Three points against Blackburn at Ewood Park in a 3–1 win but there's a double whammy for the Reds as Jamie Carragher (broken leg) and Milan Baros (broken ankle) both pick up serious injuries which rule them out for months.

SEPTEMBER 24 2003

Liverpool's UEFA Cup campaign for the season gets under way in the Slovenian capital Ljubljana. Michael Owen nets for Liverpool in a 1–1 draw and finally breaks Ian Rush's record to become LFC's greatest goalscorer in European football.

SEPTEMBER 28 2003

A thrilling match at The Valley ends in a 3–2 defeat at the hands of Charlton. Kevin Lisbie becomes the first player this season to net a hat-trick against the Reds and bags the points for the home side. Smicer and Owen score for the Reds.

30.08.03

24.09.03

04.10.03

18.10.03

OCTOBER 4 2003

Liverpool lose again to one of the big boys at Anfield, this time crashing to a 2–1 defeat to Arsenal. Harry Kewell gives the Reds a deserved lead before Edu and Robert Pires turn the game around for the Gunners. The match is also notable for the hamstring injury sustained by Michael Owen which rules him out for a few months.

OCTOBER 15 2003

Liverpool secure their path into the second round of the UEFA Cup after seeing off the challenge of Olimpija Ljubljana at Anfield. After a 1–1 draw in the first leg, the Reds hit three without reply to set up a second-round date in Romania with Steaua Bucharest.

OCTOBER 18 2003

It's misery on the South Coast for Houllier's men as old boy Patrik Berger returns to haunt his former club with the only goal of the game as Portsmouth secure a famous victory to set the Pompey chimes ringing.

OCTOBER 25 2003

Liverpool return to winning ways with an emphatic 3–1 victory over Leeds at Anfield. Owen, Murphy and Pongolle are on target for the Reds.

OCTOBER 29 2003

Liverpool come out on top in a seven-goal thriller against Blackburn Rovers to overcome their first hurdle in the season's Carling Cup. Danny Murphy, Emile Heskey (2) and Steven Gerrard net for the Reds to see off a spirited Blackburn comeback in the second half.

29.10.03

25.10.03

+ + IN 1994 ROBBIE FOWLER TOOK 4 MINUTES

09.11.03

NOVEMBER 6 2003

A boggy pitch in Bucharest doesn't stop Djimi Traore scoring his first-ever goal for Liverpool to secure a 1–1 draw in the first leg of the Reds' second-round UEFA Cup tie. In the most trying of cicumstances, this is seen as an excellent result.

NOVEMBER 9 2003

Liverpool lose again at Anfield, this time to arch-rivals Manchester United as two Ryan Giggs goals ensure all three points for Alex Ferguson's men. Harry Kewell nets a late consolation for the Reds.

DECEMBER 3 2003

Liverpool's challenge for the Carling Cup comes to a premature end as they lose to Bolton at Anfield. A last-minute Djorkaeff penalty after a foul by Salif Diao sends the Reds crashing out of the competition, thanks to a 3–2 scoreline.

DECEMBER 6 2003

With the top-three places already looking assured even at this early stage of the season, Liverpool's match at Newcastle takes on even greater significance. Both sides are expected to be the main challengers for the final Champions League place in the Premiership table. Liverpool have to settle for a 1–1 draw, despite taking the lead early on through a Danny Murphy strike. Alan Shearer nets an equaliser from the penalty spot.

DECEMBER 13 2003

Disaster for Liverpool at Anfield as Southampton produce a shock 2–1 victory. Brett Ormerod and Michael Svensson net for the Saints, while Emile Heskey's late goal is scant consolation.

06.12.03

13.12.03

00800

26.12.03

28.12.03

DECEMBER 26 2003

Christmas cheer at Anfield as the Reds make amends for their Carling Cup exit with a resounding 3–1 victory over Bolton at Anfield. Hyypia, Pongolle and Smicer are the names on the score-sheet.

DECEMBER 28 2003

Robbie Fowler becomes the latest former Red to return to haunt his former club this season, as a late goal at the City of Manchester Stadium rescues a point for his side, forcing Liverpool into having to settle for a 2–2 draw. Kewell and Baros get the goals.

JANUARY 4 2004

Liverpool survive a banana skin of a tie in deepest Somerset as they get their FA Cup campaign off to a winning start with a 2–0 win at third division outfit Yeovil Town. After surviving some first-half scares, Heskey and Murphy eventually silence the home fans with second-half strikes.

JANUARY 7 2004

Liverpool's best result of the season so far as they win 1–0 at Chelsea without injured skipper Steven Gerrard. French midfielder Bruno Cheyrou is the hero as he nets a first-half goal following a sweeping pass from Heskey.

JANUARY 17 2004

Another costly defeat for the Reds as Robbie Keane and Helder Postiga give Tottenham a 2–1 win at White Hart Lane. Harry Kewell scores late on, but, despite a concerted effort, the Reds can't find the equaliser to secure a point.

04.01.04

07.01.04

+ + JOHN BARNES GOT HIS NICKNAME 'DIGGER' WHEN FELLOW PLAYERS SPOTTED THAT HIS INITIALS WERE JCB + +

31.01.04

24.01.04

→

JANUARY 21 2004

Liverpool are forced to settle for a point at Molineux as Wolves follow in the footsteps of Manchester City to salvage a draw with a last-minute equaliser. Bruno Cheyrou looked to have scored the decisive goal, only for Kenny Miller to break Kopites' hearts with a goal after 90 minutes.

JANUARY 24 2004

Liverpool turn in their best performance of the season so far to see off the challenge of Newcastle with a 2–1 victory at Anfield to secure their passage into the fifth round of the FA Cup. Midfielder Bruno Cheyrou is again the hero as he nets both goals.

JANUARY 31 2004

Local pride remains intact for both Reds and Blues as Liverpool and Everton battle out a 0–0 draw at Anfield.

FEBRUARY 11 2004

Liverpool secure a 2–1 victory over Manchester City, with Michael Owen scoring inside the first three minutes. It's his first goal in three months, and he follows it up by helping to set up Steven Gerrard's match-winner.
.

FEBRUARY 15 2003

It looked on paper to be a home banker when Liverpool were paired with Portsmouth in the FA Cup. But full-back Matt Taylor's late equaliser to make the score 1–1 means the Reds will have to travel to Fratton Park and win at the second attempt if they are going to progress.

15.02.04

11.02.04

11.03.04

14.03.04

FEBRUARY 22 2003

The replay on the South Coast proves to be another setback in Liverpool's season as Richard Hughes scores a late winner to send the Reds crashing out. Michael Owen's penalty miss when the scores are still locked at 0–0 makes the journey back north even longer and more painful for the away fans.

MARCH 11 2004

After beating Levski Sofia in the third round of the UEFA Cup, Liverpool are given a fourth-round tie with top French outfit Marseille. The first leg ends in a 1–1 draw at Anfield, with Didier Drogba equalising Milan Baros' goal for the Reds to set up a dramatic second leg in the South of France.

MARCH 14 2004

As if Portsmouth haven't inflicted enough misery on Liverpool this season, their South Coast neighbours go and heap on more misery as Southampton secure a 2–0 victory at St Mary's to record a rare league double over Gerard Houllier's men.

MARCH 25 2004

Liverpool's UEFA Cup dream disappears against a background of 60,000 screaming Marseille fans in the Stade Velodrome. Heskey gives the Reds the lead before it all goes wrong for Liverpool as Biscan is sent off and then Drogba and Meitze score to dump them out of the competition. The cup dream is over for another season.

APRIL 4 2004

Liverpool record their most convincing win of the season so far as they thump four goals past Blackburn without reply. Maybe in the back of their minds are the two major injuries they sustained at Ewood Park earlier in the season... Whatever the motivation, Owen scores two, Heskey nets one and Todd puts one in his own net to seal the win.

25.03.04

04.04.04

09.04.04

24.04.03

APRIL 9 2004

Liverpool appear to be on the verge of becoming the first side to beat Arsenal in the league this season – until it all goes wrong in the second half. Goals from Gerrard and Owen give the Reds a 2–1 half-time lead, but a Thierry Henry-inspired Arsenal side turn it around after the break, eventually running out 4–2 winners.

APRIL 12 2004

Another Anfield defeat for the home fans to stomach as Shaun Bartlett heads into the Kop net to secure a 1–0 victory for Charlton.

APRIL 24 2004

The annual trip to Manchester United is one the players dare not lose this time if they want their dreams of finishing fourth to remain alive and kicking. Thankfully Danny Murphy is in the team. Sure enough, he scores, and Liverpool win 1–0. It's happened again, for the third time in four seasons.

MAY 8 2004

Liverpool save their best away display of the season for the final match on their travels as goals from Owen, Heskey and Gerrard secure a 3–0 win for the Reds at Birmingham. Newcastle's failure to beat Wolves the following day and then their draw with Southampton in midweek means Liverpool will definitely finish fourth.

MAY 15 2004

With Champions League qualification already assured, Liverpool enjoy their final match of the season against Newcastle free of the pressure which has been accompanying them over recent months. Shola Ameobi scores for Newcastle before Owen levels for Liverpool in the second half. It finishes 1–1, Liverpool finish in the coveted fourth position and Newcastle have to be content with fifth and a UEFA Cup place.

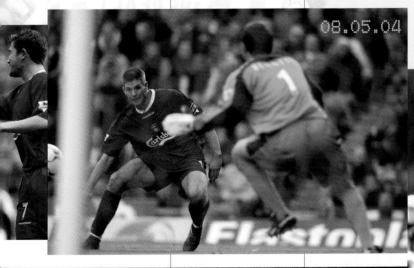

08.05.04

15.05.04

S
T
E
V
E

F
I
N
N
A
N

Capital gain

AFTER HIS FIRST SEASON, STEVE FINNAN STILL CAN'T QUITE BELIEVE HE IS PLAYING FOR LIVERPOOL. BUT AS HE ADMITS HE STILL HAS PLENTY TO PROVE

Steve Finnan still can't believe he is playing for one of the biggest clubs in world football.

The Republic of Ireland international has been at Anfield for over a year now, following his transfer from Fulham, but he says he still has to pinch himself from time to time to make sure the whole experience isn't anything more than just a wild dream.

He says, "As a kid my dream always was to play for a big club. It's what every youngster wants and I was no different. But what you dream and what you get are two different things and I honestly never thought it would come true for me.

"To think I am playing for Liverpool – one of the biggest and best-known clubs in the world – is just incredible."

Finnan's move to Anfield during the summer of 2003 closed the chapter on one of the worst-kept secrets in the game.

It had been known for some time that the young full-back was going to call time on his career at Fulham and swap London for Merseyside, where he would team-up once again with Reds' first-team coach Christian Damiano.

"I loved my time at Fulham," he says. "They're a good club with good lads and I enjoyed every minute of my career there, but when Liverpool come calling, you always have to say yes.

"I knew for a long time that Liverpool were interested in me but I didn't dare get too excited just in case nothing happened and the speculation just went away. Then when they finally told me the deal could be done I was very pleased. I was impressed with what Gerard Houllier had to tell me and I had no hesitation in signing.

"Of course the fact that Christian Damiano was already at Liverpool was a factor in my decision, but it wasn't the be-all and end-all. I'd still have signed even if I knew nobody. Christian had a big impact on my development at Fulham and I knew I'd be working with more world-class coaches at Liverpool."

Finnan, by his own admission, enjoyed an up-and-down debut season on Merseyside. Impressive when he played, he was still recuperating from an operation when he arrived at the

STEVE'S STATS FOR CLUB AND COUNTRY UP TO MAY 2004

1ST TEAM GAMES	31
1ST TEAM GOALS	0
IRELAND CAPS	25
IRELAND GOALS	0

> "I KNOW WHAT I AM CAPABLE OF AND I KNOW I CAN PERFORM WELL ENOUGH TO HOLD DOWN A PLACE IN THE SIDE WHEN I'M FULLY FIT"

club at the beginning of the season, and was often sidelined by injuries. He didn't play for a four-month spell midway through the season.

"I was disappointed to get some injuries," he said. "When you move to a new club you always want to make a good first impression and I'm not sure the fans saw the best of me last season. That's frustrating.

"I was in and out of the team at times because of injuries and that definitely held me back.

"I know that some people were saying I had done pretty well and had contributed a lot to the team from an attacking point of view, but I wanted to do better.

"I know what I am capable of and I know I can perform well enough to hold down a place in the side when I'm fully fit. Don't get me wrong, I really enjoyed my first season at Liverpool but I'm really hoping my second one can be even better, that I can enjoy an injury-free run and that I can play my part in helping the team be successful."

What about off the field? How has Finnan adapted to the lifestyle changes which come following a move from the nation's capital to the forthcoming Capital of Culture?

"I really like Liverpool," he said. "Of course I miss my family and friends from down south but I have found Liverpool to be a very welcoming city. I have definitely settled in well. I just hope my stay here can be a long and successful one."

It's been a difficult season for a player who sets himself such high standards, but he has made himself first choice for right-back in the Republic of Ireland squad for the 2006 World Cup qualifying campaign, and he should return to the Premiership side for the 2004–05 season with a renewed sense of purpose. ⊕

LIVERPOOL FOOTBALL CLUB
YOU'LL NEVER WALK ALONE
EST·1892

STEVEN GERRARD

S   T   E   V   E   N

GERRARD

+ + + STEVEN GERRARD HAS WON FOUR MAJOR TROPHIES – THE UEFA CUP, THE FA CUP AND THE WORTHINGTON CUP (TWICE) + + +

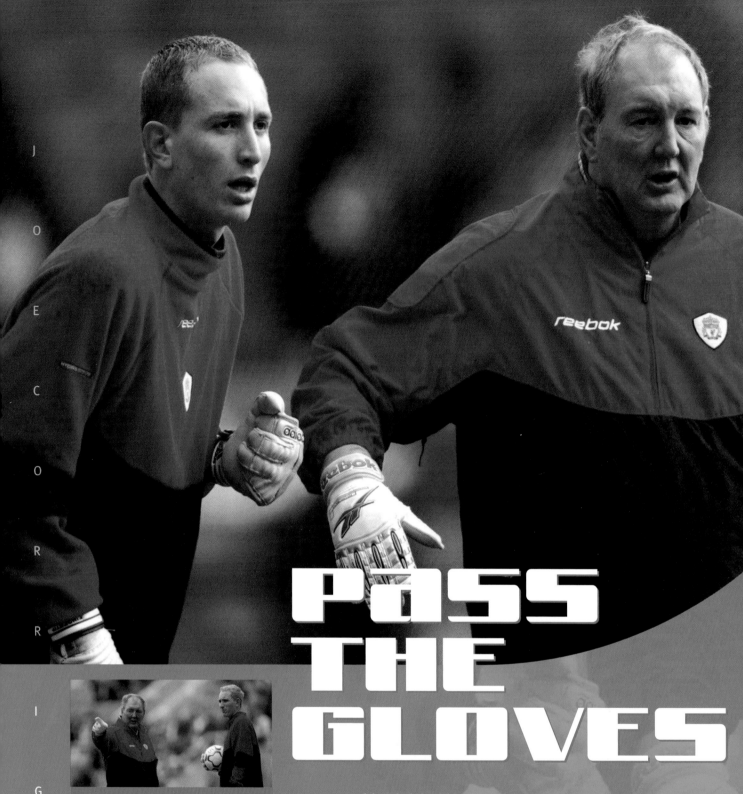

PASS THE GLOVES

JOE CORRIGAN SAYS LIVERPOOL ARE "INCREDIBLY LUCKY" TO BE ABLE TO BOAST TWO OF EUROPEAN FOOTBALL'S MOST HIGHLY RATED GOALKEEPERS

Jerzy Dudek and Chris Kirkland both signed on the same day a couple of years ago, and goalkeeping coach Corrigan says the Reds should be delighted to be able to call on the services of both men.

The battle for the number one spot at Anfield has been intriguing over recent seasons as both Dudek and Kirkland have earned spells between the sticks.

Dudek began his Anfield life as first choice ahead of Kirkland before an alarming dip in form saw his place taken by the England Under-21 star.

Sadly for Kirkland, he hasn't been able to command a regular place because of a series of injury problems, meaning Dudek has been the more regular of the two in the team over the past couple of seasons.

"We're lucky to have them both," says Corrigan. "At the top level you need at least two – and probably more – top-quality goalkeepers because injuries can strike at any time, as we have found out.

"I watched a lot of Jerzy Dudek in action for Feyenoord before we signed him and I was always impressed. It's often difficult to judge foreign keepers because you can never be totally sure they will adapt to English football, but I must say I never really doubted Jerzy.

"There were things he had to work on when he came here. For example, I never saw him catch a cross with Feyenoord. The foreign mentality is to punch crosses clear, but you'd never get away with that style over here. He also had to get used to the physical element of the Premiership because he wasn't used to strikers barging into him following crosses into the area.

"We did a lot of work in training and spent lots of time doing different sessions in a bid to help him adapt as quickly as he could. I think he has done remarkably well. He's had the odd dip, but who hasn't?

"Jerzy is a wonderful goalkeeper with a great technique. His shot-stopping is first-class and he is a pleasure to work with every day in training.

"The same can be said for Chris Kirkland, who is another goalkeeper I admire greatly. If I didn't believe in Chris then I never would have recommended that we sign him. The truth is I am sure he will be England's number one goalkeeper for many years to come in the future. He is top, top class.

"Unfortunately he has had some injury problems since he came here, but he's still very young with the majority of his career still ahead of him. He can bounce back from his setbacks and really make a name for himself.

"The first thing you notice about Chris is his size. He's a big lad and commands great presence as a goalkeeper. But he's very agile as well

and is able to throw himself around the goal as well as anybody.

"At a time when there aren't a huge amount of English goalkeepers coming through, it's nice to see someone like Chris developing into one of the best around. If it weren't for injuries then he probably would have already had several caps for his country.

"His first battle is to win the number one shirt at Liverpool and that's going to be hard enough, because Jerzy will take some shifting. The good thing about this club is that the team spirit is so good and there's no animosity between players competing for positions. There's a healthy rivalry, of course, but when Jerzy is in goal then Chris wants him to do well and vice versa.

"They are both professionals and both badly want to play, but they respect the club and understand decisions have to be made. That decision rests with the manager, but I'm sure it's a decision he relishes as it's better to have a selection problem with players to choose from than one which comes about because you're short on numbers."

> "JERZY IS A WONDERFUL GOALKEEPER WITH A GREAT TECHNIQUE. HIS SHOT-STOPPING IS FIRST-CLASS AND HE IS A PLEASURE TO WORK WITH EVERY DAY IN TRAINING"

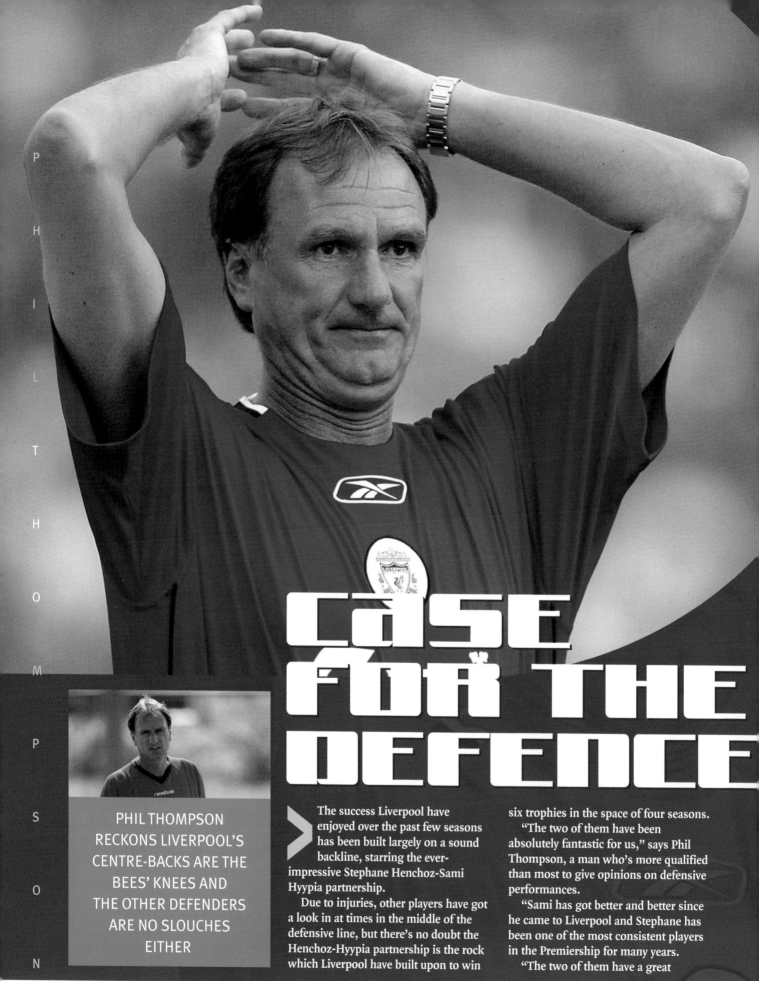

CASE FOR THE DEFENCE

PHIL THOMPSON RECKONS LIVERPOOL'S CENTRE-BACKS ARE THE BEES' KNEES AND THE OTHER DEFENDERS ARE NO SLOUCHES EITHER

> The success Liverpool have enjoyed over the past few seasons has been built largely on a sound backline, starring the ever-impressive Stephane Henchoz-Sami Hyypia partnership.

Due to injuries, other players have got a look in at times in the middle of the defensive line, but there's no doubt the Henchoz-Hyypia partnership is the rock which Liverpool have built upon to win six trophies in the space of four seasons.

"The two of them have been absolutely fantastic for us," says Phil Thompson, a man who's more qualified than most to give opinions on defensive performances.

"Sami has got better and better since he came to Liverpool and Stephane has been one of the most consistent players in the Premiership for many years.

"The two of them have a great

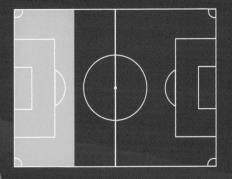

understanding of each other's game and they have both contributed enormously to what has been achieved over the last few years.

"I don't think there has been a better defensive partnership in this country over the last few years and they have both certainly enhanced their reputations across Europe for what they have done for us."

As far as Hyypia is concerned, the decision to join Liverpool is the best he has made during his career.

"I came to the Premiership as a relatively unknown player and I like to think I have done a good job for the team," he says modestly.

"I don't think we have quite reached our potential as a squad yet but I am confident we will do in time. We've had some good moments over the last few years and some not so good moments, and we all want to taste more of the good times again as soon as possible.

"It's nice if people think the partnership I have with Stephane has helped the team. I think we have a very good understanding of each other's game. It took time to gel, as all partnerships do, but over the months and years we have complemented each other well. I know where he will be during a game and what decisions he will make, and also he knows what I'm going to do. That's important for a defence."

It goes without saying, though, that Hyypia and Henchoz, good as they are, can't do all the work on their own at the back.

Full-backs Jamie Carragher and John Arne Riise, as well as Steve Finnan, are vital components in Liverpool's vision for the future.

Carragher spent five months out of the side last season but returned in time to secure himself a place in the England squad for the European Championships, while Riise recovered from a dip at the start of the season to produce his best form at Anfield since his brilliant debut season.

"While I was out of the team injured I started looking more closely at areas where my game could be improved," says Carragher.

"I know people have always said that I don't get forward enough and that is definitely an area of my game which I have worked on. I don't want to forget the fact that I'm a defender and I have a job to do at the back, but I know I can help the team as an attacking force more than I have done in the past."

As far as Norwegian Riise is concerned, Carragher is the ideal man from whom to learn his trade.

"Carra is the best defender at the club," says Riise. "Every week he performs well and that is something the rest of us have to aspire to.

"I really believe we have the basis of a very good squad here and we can certainly challenge for the title this season. We certainly don't want to let ourselves and the fans down in the same way again this time around." ✦

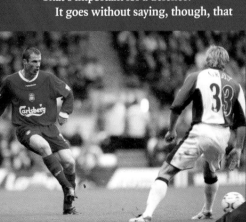

IN THE HEAT OF BATTLE

SAMMY LEE SAYS THERE ARE REASONS TO BE CHEERFUL ABOUT THE PERFORMANCES OF STEVEN GERRARD – HE BRINGS OUT THE BEST IN THOSE AROUND HIM...

When former manager Gerard Houllier was asked to comment on Steven Gerrard's performance on the last day of last season against Newcastle he was temporarily left speechless.

So good had the Reds' skipper been in the 1–1 draw with the Magpies, Houllier took time to compose his thoughts before delivering his verdict. And when it came, it was short, sweet and to the point. "He was awesome," said the Frenchman. "Absolutely awesome."

Gerrard, in the opinion of many, almost single-handedly carried Liverpool to fourth place last season with a series of inspirational midfield performances which rendered any Player of the Year awards at Anfield a formality.

At the start of the season, the Reds employed a fluent and fluid midfield system with Harry Kewell, El Hadji

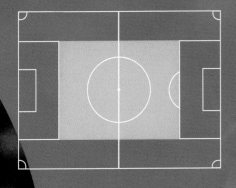

Diouf and Vladimir Smicer swapping roles at any given moment in the knowledge that Gerrard was ready and waiting behind to halt any opposition breakaway if the Reds attack broke down.

And if there's one man who knows how crucial Gerrard's presence in the side is, it's Liverpool's head coach Sammy Lee. As a former star of the Reds midfield himself, and now Sven-Goran Eriksen's assistant with England, he believes that the qualities that Gerrard brings to his national side are the ones that have been carefully instilled at Anfield. This has been especially true since Gerrard took on the responsibilties that come with the Liverpool captaincy.

"I really think Steven is a great player and has a great effect on and off the pitch. He's matured greatly over the last few years and taken to the captaincy of the club very very well. For me, knowing him as a former Liverpool player and a fan, he has been great for the club," says Lee.

During the season Liverpool were hit by injuries to key players in the midfield

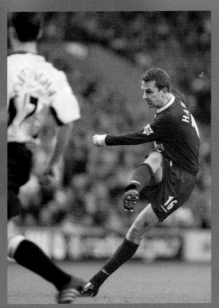

area, it was Gerrard time and again who seemed to be doing everyone's job, from tracking back and defending to charging forward in attack or even scoring goals himself.

"I had a good season but this is a team game and I don't want to take all the credit," Gerrard says. "We have some good midfielders and there's no doubt the quality is there for us to do even better, especially if the club bring in some new players during the the year.

"Didi Hamann is a great player and the reason I was able to get forward more towards the end of last season is because I know Didi can sit back and fill in for me if our attack breaks down.

"Danny Murphy also got into the team towards the end of the season and scored our winning goal again against Man United at Old Trafford. He has a happy habit of doing that.

"And, of course, Harry Kewell is going to be a big player for us. I think Harry has said he didn't do as well as he'd have liked last year, but he'll be a great player for us. I know that."

Aussie star Kewell, as Gerrard says, wasn't too happy with his debut season in the Liverpool midfield, but he's vowed to get better and better.

He says, "I haven't delivered yet like I know I can and that is very frustrating for me. I started last year well but then a couple of things went wrong for me and I couldn't really get back to my best form.

"Some people said to me that these things happen and they wanted to make excuses. But I don't go along with that. I set high standards for myself and I intend to deliver this season."

Promising words from the Aussie maestro's mouth indeed. One thing is for sure, if he can complement the world-class performances of Steven

Gerrard, then Liverpool's Championship charge for this season will certainly have a chance of ending happily.

"We want to be challenging the top three," says Gerrard. "Fourth was necessary last season for lots of reasons, but this year we want to do a whole lot better and go as high as we can."

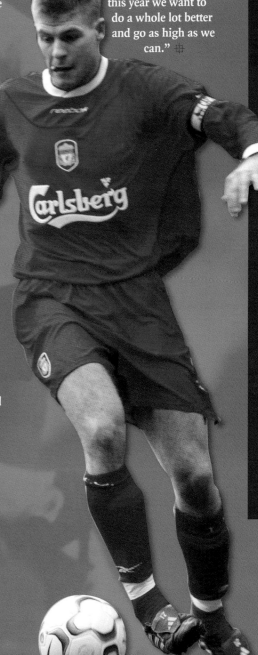

IAN RUSH – ANFIELD HERO

GOALS WIN GAMES

LIVERPOOL LEGEND IAN RUSH RECKONS THE REDS HAVE THE STRIKING POWER TO FIRE THEM TOWARDS SUCCESS IN THE FUTURE

> Ian Rush, the former Anfield goal machine, is a regular face down at Melwood these days where he is passing on to the club's current strikers the benefit of his vast experience in mastering the greatest art of all in football – scoring goals.

Rush admits he had no hesitation in accepting Gerard Houllier's offer of part-time work at Melwood and he insists there is more than enough quality within the striking ranks at Anfield to be confident of success over the coming years.

He says, "The gaffer asked me if I wanted to join the staff as a striker coach and it was an opportunity I couldn't turn down. Liverpool was my club as a player and the opportunity to come and work here again was far too tempting to refuse.

"All I try to do during every session is

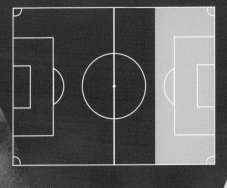

pass on some of the tips I learned as a player and hope the lads here find them of some use.

"You can't really teach scoring goals as it's a talent you are either born with or you're not, but you can teach movement in the area and how to find space to create chances for yourself.

"I'm really enjoying working here. It's a great thrill for me to be out on the training field working with top-quality players.

"I always knew that I might fancy going into coaching when my playing days came to an end and thankfully one or two doors have opened for me at both club and international level."

So what does Rushie make of the current crop of Anfield attackers? There's a top England forward in Michael Owen, a Czech star in the shape of Milan Baros and a young French starlet in Florent Sinama Pongolle. Then add to this the recent arrival of another Frenchman, Djibril Cisse, who scored 26 for Auxerre last season, and the Liverpool attack is looking very healthy. What can Rush tell us?

"Firstly, they are all excellent players in different ways. At a top club, if you want to be successful, then you need a blend of strikers who can work well together and we have that at Liverpool.

"Everyone knows about Michael Owen. What else is there to say except he is one of the best in the business. I never cease to be amazed by how he overcomes the pressures which come with being Michael Owen to regularly produce the goods on the pitch.

"When he first came onto the first-team scene he was all about pace. He is so quick and he scared defenders to death. Now teams have worked out how to play against quick strikers, and so he needed to learn and improve other aspects of his game, and he's done it. He scores goals from more positions now, he can shoot with his left foot and he's not bad in the air for a small lad either.

"He has his critics, because it's always a story when Michael Owen doesn't score, but he never lets it get to him and he always bounces back. That's the sign of a great player.

"Milan Baros is a star of the future. He came to Liverpool as a young lad from the Czech Republic and it took him a while to find his feet and to settle in. To be fair to him though, he has done really well.

"When you go to a new country and don't speak the language then it's hard. I know that from personal experience. But Milan has knuckled down and I think he has made a real impact.

"There are areas of his game he can improve upon, of course, but he has bags of raw talent and ability. He is only going to get better and better.

Rush says that Cisse — who missed Euro 2004 — was champing at the bit to make his Premiership debut, and find out how he would fare at the top level of the English game.

"By the time pre-season came along, he was desperate to get going."

"Finally, Florent Sinama Pongolle is definitely another one to look out for. I think we beat off competition from a lot of European clubs to bring him here and it's easy to see why.

"Like Baros, he is only a young lad and needs time to learn and develop his skills, but he has a great eye for goal and is certainly another one to watch in the future.

"He has probably played more first-team games than he thought he would this early into his Liverpool career, but that will only stand him in good stead for the future. He's settling in well at Liverpool and I can see a time soon when he is regularly banging on the first-team door."

3

1 I was signed from Feyenoord and I am the son of a Polish miner.

2 I sustained a cruciate knee ligament injury in January 2003 and I was ruled out of Euro 2004 with a broken wrist.

3 I scored my first goal for Liverpool against Aston Villa at the Kop end when I was wearing number 23. I haven't scored too many since.

Guess Who?

CAN YOU IDENTIFY THE LFC STARS FROM THESE TEASING FACTS?

2

4 I was signed from a little-known Dutch club but have since established myself as one of the top players in my position in Europe.

5 Liverpool are the second Premiership team I have played for after I decided to move to Anfield from Ewood Park.

6 I wear squad number 25 at Anfield and last season played in a new position, centre-half.

7

7 I was signed from Monaco and I turned down a move to Fulham to join Liverpool. I have scored goals against both Everton and Manchester United.

9 I scored the last-ever goal at the old Wembley for my country in a famous victory over England. I've scored a few crackers for Liverpool too.

10 I switched squad number at the start of season 2003–04 to allow Harry Kewell to take the number he wanted.

11 I've scored three winning goals at Old Trafford and was voted Player of the Year at Liverpool at the end of the 2002–03 season.

12 I turned down a move to Manchester United to sign for Liverpool and scored 11 goals in my debut season.

8 I made my Anfield debut against Blackburn Rovers after Gerard Houllier noticed me playing in an Academy game and asked me to join the first-team squad at Melwood.

13 I scored on my debut in 1997 and have also scored two goals in FA Cup finals. I'm Liverpool's leading goalscorer in European competitions.

14 I joined Liverpool in the summer of 2003, but my potential was first spotted by Le Havre in 1992 when I was just eight years old. I made 23 appearances in my first season with the Reds.

15 I was once dubbed the 'Ostravan Maradona' and scored on my full debut for Liverpool at Bolton.

All answers on page 63

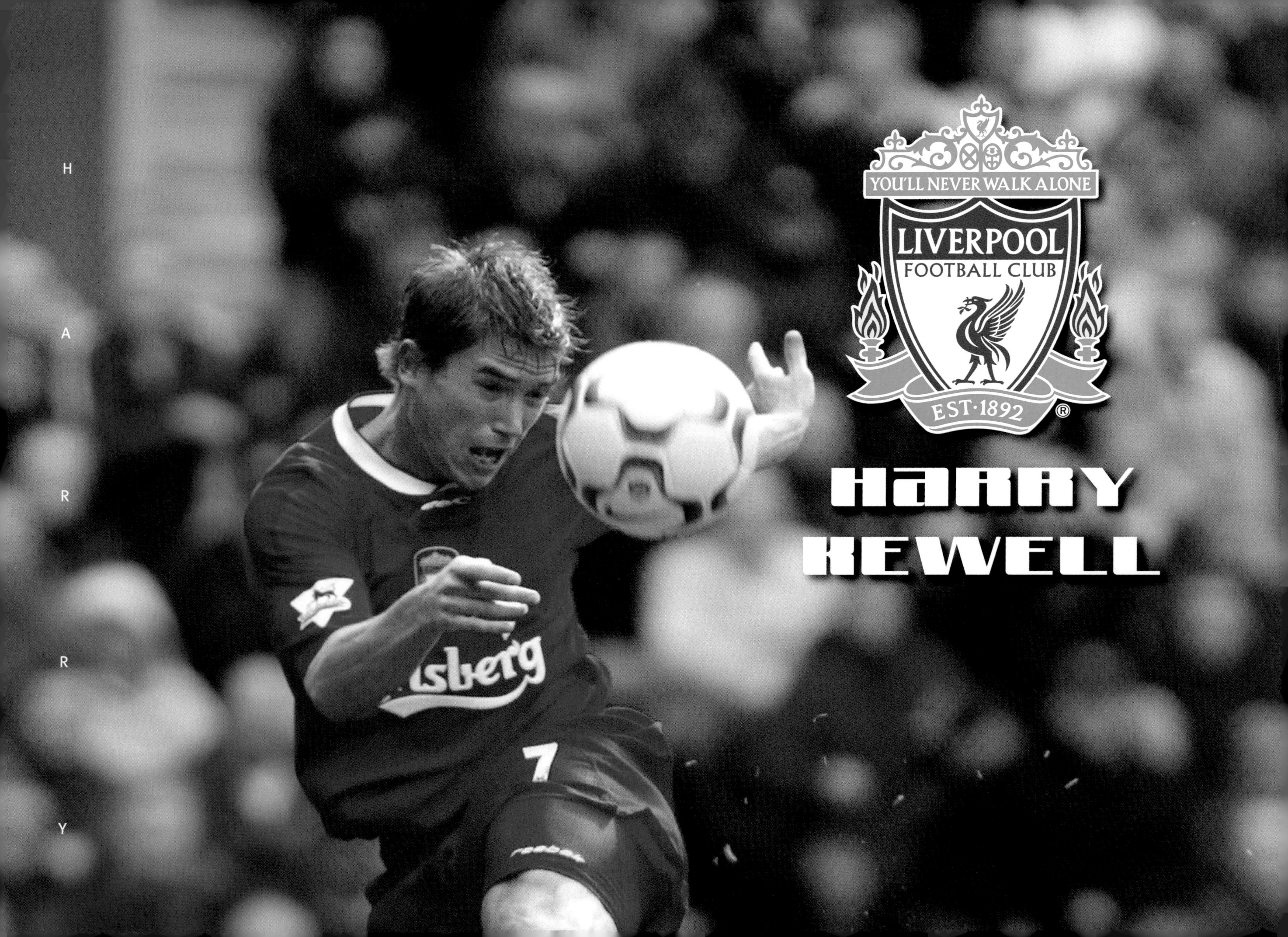

LIVERPOOL FOOTBALL CLUB
YOU'LL NEVER WALK ALONE
EST·1892

HARRY KEWELL

H   A   R   R   Y

+ + HARRY KEWELL WAS 'DISCOVERED' BY EX-LEEDS MANAGER HOWARD WILKINSON AT THE NEW SOUTH WALES FOOTBALL ACADEMY + +

LIVERPOOL

Welsh Wizard
Ian Rush was Liverpool's
greatest-ever goalscorer

5

HISTORY

1. In which year were Liverpool formed?
   a) 1782 b) 1892 c) 1902

2. How many European Cups have Liverpool won?
   a) 3 b) 4 c) 5

3. In which year did Liverpool last win the title?
   a) 1990 b) 1991 c) 1992

4. What is Liverpool's record crowd?
   a) 61,905 b) 62,766 c) 63,109

5. How many European goals did Ian Rush score for Liverpool?
   a) 18 b) 19 c) 20

CURRENT SQUAD

6. What squad number did Harry Kewell wear last season?
   a) 7 b) 17 c) 27

7. On which date in May was Steven Gerrard born?
   a) 18 b) 24 c) 30

8. Add together Florent Sinama Pongolle's and Anthony Le Tallec's squad numbers last season and what do you get?
   a) 42 b) 43 c) 44

9. How many games did it take Michael Owen to score his first Liverpool goal?
   a) 1 b) 2 c) 3

10. How many millions did Liverpool spend on Emile Heskey?
    a) 9 b) 10 c) 11

14

Macca spent nine years with the Reds

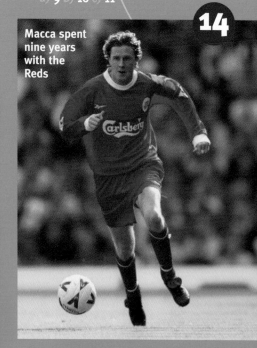

4

Bill Shankly had a unique rapport with fans

BY NUMBERS

13

Fowler was one of the great natural finishers

GOALS AND GLORY

16. How many goals has Markus Babbel scored for Liverpool?
a) 4 b) 5 c) 6

17. How many goals did Michael Owen score for England in the 2002 World Cup?
a) 2 b) 3 c) 4

18. Who has made the most league appearances for Liverpool?
a) Callaghan b) Hunt c) St John

19. Robbie Fowler once scored a hat-trick against Arsenal in how many minutes?
a) 2 b) 4 c) 8

20. How many goals did Jerzy Dudek concede on his Liverpool debut?
a) 2 b) 3 c) 4

MISCELLANEOUS

11. What is Liverpool's longest sequence of unbeaten games from the start of a season?
a) 28 b) 29 c) 30

12. How many goals did Liverpool score in their record league win?
a) 7 b) 9 c) 11

13. How many goals did Robbie Fowler score in the 2001 UEFA Cup final?
a) 1 b) 2 c) 3

14. What was Steve McManaman's squad number at Anfield?
a) 15 b) 16 c) 17

15. How many times did Sami Hyypia appear for Liverpool in the 2003–04 season, making him the most regular face in the team?
a) 48 b) 51 c) 52

Ian Callaghan was LFC's Mr Consistency

18

All answers on page 63

YOUNG GUNS HEADING FOR GLORY

P

O

N

G

O

L

L

E

I knew when I signed for Liverpool that I would be competing for a place in the team alongside some of the great strikers in the game. But that challenge didn't daunt me because I knew I would have a chance of making it if I kept working hard.

To be honest I'm a bit surprised that I played so many games last season, because I know the manager said I would probably spend a year or so playing in the reserves and then gradually move up to the first team in good time.

I played a lot more than I expected last year and I think I gave a good account of myself overall. I certainly don't feel as though I let myself down and I know from speaking to the fans that they can see something in me.

As a striker I know you are judged on the amount of goals you score and so it was pleasing for me to be on the score sheet a few times. I know I can score goals in the Premiership and I know I can contribute to this Liverpool team.

On the whole, I was pleased with my performances for Liverpool when I was involved last year. I'm the kind of player who relies a lot on speed and the fact I won some penalties for the team maybe says that defenders didn't know much about me.

That's a good thing. But I also know that the more I play, the more they'll learn about me and that is something I will have to take on board and adapt to.

I'm excited by the future here and I know I have definitely made the right move coming to Liverpool. ⊕

PONGOLLE...

> French gems Florent Sinama Pongolle and Anthony Le Tallec have now spent a year on Merseyside adapting to life in Premiership football. How well do they think they have done so far and how much have they still to offer? Let's find out...

I feel as though I made a good start to my Liverpool career but then over the second half of the season I picked up a couple of injuries and that held me back a bit.

Like Pongo, I was expecting a year of reserve team football to start with. It's always hard coming to a new league and, although we were told what to expect in terms of the speed and physical demands of the Premiership, it's not until you get here and start playing that you realise how different it is.

Over the first few months of the season I made some appearances for the first team and really enjoyed myself. I found it tough but at the same time I didn't feel out of my depth at all. I got a lot of confidence from those early months, but then I started to be a bit unlucky with injuries and I couldn't really end the season on a high.

I expect a lot from myself in this coming season. I'm a young player but there are lots of young players playing in the Premiership. I want to prove myself again and show the boss I can do a job for him in the team. ⊕

GERARD HOULLIER'S VIEW:
It's well-documented that I was delighted to see both Le Tallec and Pongolle and that we had to beat off stiff competition from some of the top clubs in Europe to get them. I have to be honest and admit the speed with which they took to the game in this country did surprise me. I thought they would need a good six months to a year to get used to English football before we could even consider them for the first team. The fact that both players have made a fair amount of appearances already tells you everything about their desire to succeed and do well here. They have surprised me, for sure, but I also know what they have to offer and I can tell you they will continue getting better and better over the coming years.

LE TALLEC 20

L E T A L L E C

E
U
R
O
P
E
A
N
N

LIVERPOOL'S GREAT EUROPEAN NIGHTS

IN THEIR QUEST FOR SILVERWARE, LIVERPOOL FC HAVE TRAVELLED THE LENGTH AND BREADTH OF EUROPE, WINNING NINE MAJOR TROPHIES. HERE ARE FIVE OF THE MOST MEMORABLE MATCHES

EUROPEAN CUP FINAL – MAY 25 1977, ROME

LIVERPOOL 3-1 BORUSSIA MOENCHENGLADBACH
MCDERMOTT
SMITH
NEAL (Pen)

Liverpool won their first European Cup on a never-to-be-forgotten night in Italy's eternal city.

Having disposed of FC Zurich in the semi-final, they were overwhelming favourites to lift the cup despite facing opposition of real quality.

The outcome of the tie was rarely in doubt after Terry McDermott latched onto a defence-splitting pass from Steve

Heighway to drive the ball into the net midway through the first half.

Borussia equalised soon after the half-time break when Simonsen capitalised

on an error by Case to lash the ball past Clemence, but Liverpool always looked capable of stepping up a gear and it came as no surprise when they regained the lead after Smith headed Heighway's corner into the roof of the net to score a rare goal.

Liverpool's victory was secure when Keegan was upended in the area and Neal stroked home the penalty to ensure the Reds lifted Europe's premier trophy for the first time in their history.

Team: Clemence, Neal, Jones, Smith, Kennedy, Hughes, Keegan, Case, Heighway, Callaghan, McDermott.

I
G
H
T
S

EUROPEAN CUP FINAL – MAY 10 1978, LONDON

LIVERPOOL 1-0 FC BRUGES
DALGLISH

Probably one of the cagiest European finals for many years, but Liverpool fans who made the trip to Wembley didn't care as they celebrated watching their side successfully defend the trophy to reinforce their position as the continent's number one club.

Bruges were happy to adopt negative tactics and hope to nick a goal on the break – or even to take the tie to penalties – but one piece of magic from Kenny Dalglish scuppered their dreams

and ensured the Reds were celebrating for the second successive year.

The decisive goal came in the wake of an immaculately-weighted ball from Souness into Dalglish's path and, as the goalkeeper advanced, Liverpool's number seven clipped a glorious shot into the far corner of the goal.

Amazingly, Bruges almost nicked an equaliser late on when Phil Thompson was forced to clear off his own line, but that was the only scare on another memorable night for Bob Paisley's men.

Team: Clemence, Neal, Thompson, Hansen, Kennedy, Hughes, Dalglish, Case (Heighway), Fairclough, McDermott, Souness.

LIVERPOOL 1-0 REAL MADRID
KENNEDY

Liverpool had to wait three, long years before adding to their European trophy haul, but it proved to be well worth it as full-back Alan Kennedy smashed the ball into the roof of the Real Madrid net to become a hero on Merseyside.

Kennedy's moment of glory arrived nine minutes from the end of a fairly dour match, in which both sides were prepared to cancel each other out for fear of making that one costly mistake.

Dalglish and Kennedy had gone close in the early stages before Real Madrid came back into the match to enjoy some good moments of their own.

The match appeared to be heading inexorably towards extra-time when Kennedy cut in from the left after a quickly-taken throw-in and arrowed a rising shot into the far corner of the Madrid net.

Cue wild celebrations from the thousands of Liverpool fans inside the stadium as Kennedy wrote himself into Anfield folklore. Little did he know he would repeat the trick three years later.

Team: Clemence, Neal, A Kennedy, Thompson, R Kennedy, Hansen, Dalglish (Case), Lee, Johnson, McDermott, Souness.

LIVERPOOL 1-1 ROMA (Liverpool win 4-2 on penalties)
NEAL

That Liverpool beat the Italian giants of AS Roma is one thing – that they did so on Roma's home pitch was nothing short of sensational. Liverpool had enjoyed some spectacular successes over the years, but beating Roma to lift the biggest trophy in European football for a fourth time perhaps topped the lot.

When Phil Neal opened the scoring after 15 minutes, the Reds were on their way to one of their finest-ever results.

Unfortunately, they couldn't hold onto the lead and Pruzzi equalised for the home side with a close-range header, but Liverpool didn't let their heads drop and eventually forced the tie to a penalty shoot-out. Steve Nicol blazed the first kick over for Liverpool, then De Barlotemi netted for Roma. Neal equalised, Conti missed and Souness scored... 2–1 to Liverpool. Righetti levelled. Rush scored... 3–2 to the Reds. When Graziani shot over, it was left to Alan Kennedy – also the hero in Madrid – to win the Cup for Liverpool. He didn't fail – a well-executed shot into the left-hand corner of the net gave the Reds their fourth European Cup.

Team: Grobbelaar, Neal, Kennedy, Lawrenson, Whelan, Hansen, Dalglish (Robinson), Lee, Rush, Johnston (Nicol), Souness.

LIVERPOOL 5-4 ALAVES
BABBEL, GERRARD, MCALLISTER FOWLER, GELI (OG)

Perhaps one of the greatest European finals ever as Gerard Houllier won his first European trophy as Liverpool manager to complete an unprecedented treble of Worthington Cup, FA Cup and UEFA Cup in the same season.

Liverpool had waited 17 years to win a European trophy, and looked like gaining an easy victory when Babbel and Gerrard established an early 2–0 lead, but an Alaves goal from Alonso before the break suddenly gave the match a different complexion.

When McAllister netted a penalty, Liverpool again seemed to be cruising. After the break their Spanish opponents hit back, with Moreno netting twice in three minutes to level the scores at 3–3. Sub Robbie Fowler then put Liverpool 4–3 up before Cruyff levelled with one minute remaining. In extra-time Alaves were reduced to nine men when two of their players were sent off, which prompted Liverpool to go on and win the Cup as McAllister's free-kick was headed into his own goal by defender Geli. Great game. Great result.

Team: Westerveld, Babbel, Henchoz (Smicer), Hyypia, Carragher, Gerrard, Hamann, McAllister, Murphy, Owen (Berger), Heskey (Fowler).

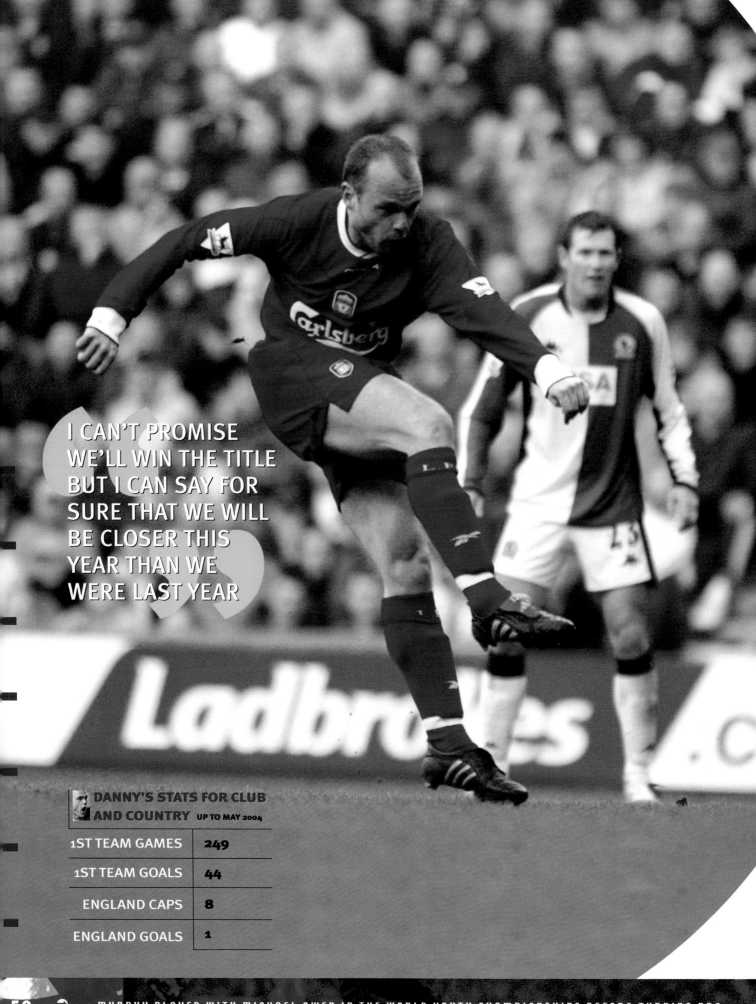

"I CAN'T PROMISE WE'LL WIN THE TITLE BUT I CAN SAY FOR SURE THAT WE WILL BE CLOSER THIS YEAR THAN WE WERE LAST YEAR"

DANNY'S STATS FOR CLUB AND COUNTRY UP TO MAY 2004

1ST TEAM GAMES	249
1ST TEAM GOALS	44
ENGLAND CAPS	8
ENGLAND GOALS	1

Moving on up

DANNY MURPHY IS SURE LIVERPOOL CAN BUILD ON FOURTH PLACE IN THE PREMIERSHIP AND DO SOMETHING SPECIAL — AT HOME AND IN THE CHAMPIONS LEAGUE — THIS SEASON

Danny Murphy has admitted the pressure is on everyone at Anfield to ensure this season is much more rewarding than the last campaign.

Murphy admits qualification for this season's Champions League was scant reward for their efforts last year and he knows the weight of expectation on the shoulders of the players to produce a title challenge has increased this season.

He says: "Last year was disappointing and we can't hide that. We finished fourth but that isn't good enough for this club. We're not one of the lesser teams in this league. We're one of the big boys and we have to prove it again this year.

"Finishing fourth was important last year because it gave us a route back into the Champions League which is where we all want to be. But as a long-term goal it's not really acceptable and we need to be setting our sights a lot higher.

"I know we can do better and I think we will this season. We certainly have the squad capable of getting closer to the top three and that's definitely our aim. Arsenal played some of the best football I have ever seen last season and deservedly won the title, but we know we're not really 30 points worse than them. The league table suggested otherwise last

year and that's why we need to work hard to close that gap.

"Getting closer is the aim and we have to believe we can do it. If we didn't believe that then what would be the point of playing through the season? The quality is here, the desire is definitely here, and I can promise we'll all be doing our best to improve this year.

"I can't promise we'll win the title but I can say for sure that we will be closer this year than we were last year."

Liverpool's chances of success this season will once again rest largely on the shoulders of captain Steven Gerrard.

The Reds skipper carried the team almost single-handedly at times last season to the coveted final Champions League place, and Murphy is fulsome in his praise for his friend and team-mate.

"Steven has been exceptional of late," he says. "He is on a different plain to everyone else at the club at the moment. I would say he and Vieira are the best two midfield players in the country right now.

"He came second in the player of the year awards last season, despite the fact he was in a team which wasn't in the Champions League and was struggling in the Premiership. That says everything about his performances.

"He can do everything. He can pass, tackle, shoot, create goals and score goals. I don't really know how he can improve because he seems to be the complete player. Players like him deserve

to be in the Champions League and I'm pleased he's going to get the chance along with the rest of us this season."

Murphy himself was Liverpool's player of the season for 2002–03, before a slip in form meant he was not even assured of a regular place last season.

The Liverpool midfielder, so disappointed to miss out on a place in England's Euro 2004 squad, is determined to ensure he returns to top form this season.

"I'm a confidence player and I think I need to have a run of games in the side to get to my best level," he explains. "I was a bit in and out last season and that was disappointing for me.

"Every year I set myself the same target and that is to work hard, to improve as a player and to progress from the standards that I set myself the previous year.

"We all know that this season is a big one for everyone at the club. It's massive and we are well aware of the need to deliver for the fans.

"The supporters have always been great with the team and have always backed us, even through the bad spells. Now is the time for us to give them something back. We all want to win trophies and to be successful and I can assure all the fans that we'll do our best over the coming months to make sure we have something more to celebrate at the end of the season." ⊕

P
U
Z
Z
L
E
P
A
G
E
S

IT ALL ADDS UP...

IF YOU KNOW YOUR 2003–04 SQUAD NUMBERS, YOU SHOULD BE ABLE TO DO THE SIMPLE TESTS
BELOW. THE ANSWER EACH TIME IS A NUMBER WHICH LEADS YOU TO A LIVERPOOL PLAYER

Steven Gerrard + Michael Owen − Stephane Henchoz = ...

John Arne Riise + Milan Baros − Michael Owen + Milan Baros = ...

Chris Kirkland + Dietmar Hamann − Bruno Cheyrou = ...

Anthony Le Tallec ÷ Michael Owen X Harry Kewell + Stephane Henchoz = ...

Neil Mellor − Steve Finnan ÷ Steve Finnan = ...

Sami Hyypia ÷ Jerzy Dudek + Steven Gerrard = ...

WHO AM I?

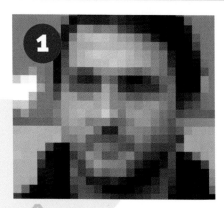

1

I came from Monaco on a free
transfer in July 2002. I am French
and my squad number is 39. I play
in goal and I came on as a sub
against Chelsea last season.

My name is...

My Senegal team-mate at Liverpool
is El-Hadji Diouf and I came to
Anfield from French side Sedan.

2

My name is...

QUICKFIRE QUESTIONS

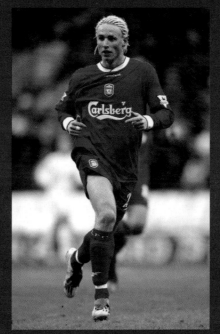

1. Who scored Liverpool's first goal last season?

2. Which teams did the double over Liverpool last season?

3. Which Liverpool player spent last season on loan with Blackburn?

4. Neil Mellor scored how many goals for the reserves last season?

5. Pongolle and Le Tallec both signed from which French club?

6. Which Liverpool players were named by Pele in the top 125 in the world?

7. How many Liverpool players were sent off in the Premiership last season?

8. How many times have Liverpool won the title?

9. When did the Reds last celebrate winning the championship?

10. Who has scored most goals for Liverpool in Europe?

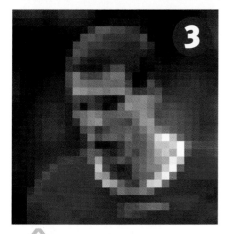

I am a left-sided midfield player and arrived at Liverpool from Lille. I scored four goals last season, two of them in an FA Cup tie at Anfield.

My name is...

I was named Norway's 'Athlete of the Year' in 2001 and I've got a contract to stay with Liverpool through until 2007.

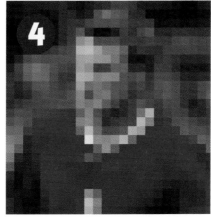

My name is...

All answers on page 63

WITH A TRADITION STRETCHING BACK MORE THAN A HUNDRED YEARS, LIVERPOOL ARE THE

ARE YOU FAN

Liverpool lift the
European Cup at
Wembley, 1978

■ How many European Cups have Liverpool won?

■ In which year did Bill Shankly resign from Liverpool?

■ From which club did Liverpool sign Oyvind Leonhardsen?

■ Against which team did Michael Owen score his first Liverpool goal?

■ How many goals did Ian Rush score in the 1986 FA Cup final?

■ Who is Liverpool's most-capped player?

■ Who has made the most appearances for the Reds?

■ The Spion Kop is named after a hill in which country?

◆ + + + + ROGER HUNT SCORED A RECORD FIVE HAT-TRICKS FOR LIVERPOOL IN THE 1961–62 SEASON + + + +

MOST SUCCESSFUL BRITISH CLUB SIDE EVER, BUT HOW MUCH DO YOU KNOW ABOUT THEM?

ENOUGH?

- Liverpool's record attendance came against which team?

- What nationality was Glen Hysen?

- Who was Kenny Dalglish's first signing for Liverpool?

- In which year were Liverpool last relegated?

- Who did Bill Shankly describe as his 'Colossus'?

- When did the fans in the Kop first sing 'You'll Never Walk Alone?'

- How many Czechs played for Liverpool in 2003–04?

- In which city did Liverpool win the European Cup in 1981?

- Who was Liverpool's manager before Bill Shankly?

- Stan Collymore left Liverpool to join which club?

- Who was the last player to score in front of a standing Kop?

- Michael Owen's 100th goal for the Reds came against which team?

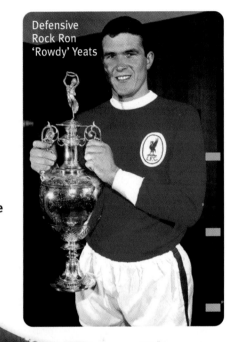

Defensive Rock Ron 'Rowdy' Yeats

All-time Great Ian Rush

Midfield General Steve McMahon

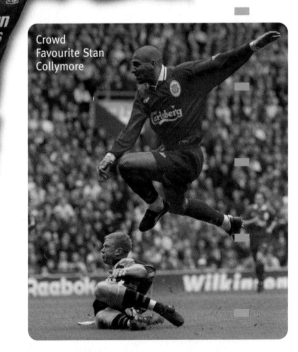

Crowd Favourite Stan Collymore

TIP FOR THE TOP

WITH STARS ARRIVING FROM EVERY CORNER OF THE GLOBE TO PLAY IN THE PREMIERSHIP, IT'S GETTING HARDER AND HARDER TO BREAK INTO THE FIRST TEAM OF A BIG ENGLISH CLUB. BUT IF YOU WANT TO SUCCEED, THE FIRST THING YOU NEED IS CONFIDENCE, AND LIVERPOOL YOUNGSTER JOHN WELSH HAS GOT THAT IN SPADES

Liverpool youngster John Welsh still reckons he has what it takes to make the breakthrough at Anfield.

Welsh has enjoyed another fantastic season for the reserves, during which he has comfortably been the Reds' most consistent performer, but he admits to a slight sense of frustration that he hasn't yet been able to force his way into first-team plans on a regular basis.

The England youth international isn't too downhearted though, and believes the chance he is looking for could be just around the corner.

He says: "If I didn't think a chance was going to come or if I didn't believe I was good enough, there wouldn't be much point in staying here. I am confident in my ability to play in the Premiership and I want to prove that at Liverpool.

"I was hoping I may have had more chances by now but at a club this size you know it is always going to be difficult because they have millions of pounds to spend on top players in the transfer market. Maybe if I was with another club I would have had a few more games under my belt,

player just by working alongside the squad we have here in training every day.

"I am very ambitious and I want to have a good career in the game. I'd love to be a success at Liverpool and I still believe I will be one day. It's going to be hard, I'm under no illusions about that. I play in the same position as Steven Gerrard, so it's clearly going to be difficult to get a place in the team, but if I do enough to impress when chances come along then maybe I can start to figure more and more in the squad and take it from there."

Despite harbouring ambitions of pursuing a career at Anfield, Welsh admits he may consider moving away for a short spell on loan if it means he will get to play first-team football more regularly.

He says: "A few of the young lads here have gone on loan to other clubs and they've benefited from it. The manager has said that's something we can look at if an offer comes in and it's definitely something I'd be interested in. To play week after week in a lower league would help me and I'm sure the coaching staff at Liverpool would keep an eye on how I was getting on, and keep up to date with my performances.

"There was a chance I could have gone on loan last season but I broke my toe and was out for a number of weeks. That was a bit of a setback for me because it came at a bad time, but these things happen in football."

Welsh's dynamism and energy in midfield have been consistent factors in the performances of Liverpool's reserve team over the last couple of seasons, and second-string boss Hugh McAuley has nothing but praise for his Liverpool-born midfielder.

Hugh says: "John has done really well. He's very consistent and that's the best thing you can say about him. He works very hard in training, he takes on board everything he's told and then he goes and puts it into practice during a match.

"His level of consistency is top class. He can tackle, run with the ball, set up chances and shoot. Maybe he could score one or two more goals but there are always areas where players can improve. I would say he has a good future in the game, hopefully at Liverpool. He's a good lad to work with and an excellent player on the field. He's getting better and better all the time for us." ⊕

⊙ + + CAPTAIN OF THE RESERVES, WELSH HAS BEEN A LIVERPOOL FAN SINCE CHILDHOOD, AND JOINED THE CLUB WHEN HE WAS JUST 10 + + ◑

57

COMPETITION FOR PLACES IS VITAL AT A CLUB LIKE LIVERPOOL AND, EVEN THOUGH THEY ARE THE BEST OF FRIENDS, FIT-AGAIN CHRIS KIRKLAND IS DETERMINED TO TAKE THE SHIRT BACK OFF JERZY DUDEK IF HE CAN

Fit for line duties

> Chris Kirkland has vowed to make this season the one when he finally lives up to his reputation as the best young goalkeeper in English football.

Kirkland not only missed much of last season with Liverpool after a series of unfortunate injury setbacks, he also saw his dreams of representing England in the European Championships dashed following an untimely wrist injury.

The young goalkeeper knows his first task this season is to prove his fitness and then dislodge Jerzy Dudek as Liverpool's undisputed number one, but he wants to at least be given a chance of achieving his ambitions by staying healthy.

Kirkland says: "I don't want to be labelled as injury-jinxed but I suppose at the moment my record of being fit hasn't been a good one.

"It's not even as if I'm picking up run-of-the-mill injuries which just keep me out for a couple of weeks. If I get injured, it always seems to be that I've broken something – whether it be my wrist or my finger last season or a cruciate knee ligament injury the year before.

"It's very frustrating and I'd be lying if I said it didn't get me down. Of course it does. I'm a young player at one of the biggest clubs around and I'm desperate to show everyone what I can do. Hopefully this season will be a better one for me. I'm so eager to play."

Kirkland would almost certainly have been in England's plans for the summer Championships in Portugal if the fates hadn't conspired against him once again, but he doesn't like to dwell on that fact for too long and instead looks positively forward to the future.

He says: "It's every English player's dream to play for their country and I'm no different. It's hard to talk about the European Championships because I don't know if I'd have been in the squad or not anyway. I don't want to take anything for granted.

"The good thing from my point of view is that I'm still young and hopefully have a lot of international tournaments still to aim for in my career.

"The most important thing for now is to make sure I play as many games as possible for Liverpool. I've had a taste of first-team action at Anfield and there's nothing I like better than playing for the first team with so many great players.

"Maybe my career here hasn't gone as I would have liked in an ideal world so far but, as I said, there's still plenty of time for that to change and for my fortunes to take a turn for the better.

"I know I have another big test ahead of me to win the battle with Jerzy Dudek for the position in goal but that's the sort of challenge I'm going to enjoy. It's certainly a nicer challenge than having to win a battle against injury.

"I've had enough of those sort of battles to last me a lifetime and now I want to have a good run clear of injuries to try and start living up to my potential." ⊕

YOU'LL NEVER WALK ALONE
LIVERPOOL
FOOTBALL CLUB
EST·1892
SAMI
HYYPIA
S
A
M
I
H